To that kid within each and every one of us
who forever knows no limits

Copyright © 2020 by Connor Berryhill

All rights reserved. No part of this book may be reproduced or used in any manner without written permission of the copyright owner except for the use of quotations in a book review. For more information, address: connor@microactivist.org

THIRD EDITION
ISBN: 9780982518854

Authors: Connor & Mazi Berryhill
Contact: Connor@MicroActivist.org

www.MicroActivist.org

Buy for your whole group and save big!
Bulk discount available.

WHY WE NEEDED TO WRITE THIS BOOK

Creating this book has been my passion and my therapy. I was born obsessed with water. Baths, pools, puddles... you name it, I was in it! Then I visited the ocean and fell in love. The amazing creatures I met there became my family. As I grew, this aquatic world remained my safe happy place, while topside I struggled to fit in. During school lunches, other kids babbled on about the latest video games, while I stared, confused and saddened by their lack of interest in discussing my beloved ocean documentaries.

Concerned, the big people ran a battery of tests that revealed I was highly gifted and also autistic. This meant my gift came with social disabilities that could make fitting in a lifelong challenge. My parents did a lot of heavy thinking, and made the difficult decision to place me on a more radical path than the one laid before us. They shifted the focus away from my shortcomings and instead did everything in their power to support my ocean passion. They had faith that by empowering the thing I cared about most, it would ignite my "superpowers" and help me overcome the many challenges I faced... .and it seems to be working.

Today, it's my passion that drives me to teach other kids about the ocean, along with finding new ways to connect and share the deep love I have for all things aquatic. Now that my little whirlwind of a sister has joined in, we're unstoppable!

Writing this first book is part of our ongoing fight to save our ocean family, and a story about the dangers of balloons just made sense. Our beloved adopted pigeon, "Lucky," was rescued from a tangle of balloons. We're creating this book to help protect all the animals like Lucky who fall victim to carelessly released balloons.

Connor, age 4, begins his lifelong commitment to support ocean animals.

It was a pretty standard day for us, full of scuba diving, whale riding, and saving animals...
the usual stuff for kids like us.
My little sis Mazi and I help protect the ocean.

We're MicroActivists.

That's Mazi down there in the boat, patrolling with our animal pals. And that's me atop that adorable whale. His name is Kerchunk.

Balloons!
To be released from a wedding!
So what's wrong with balloons, you might ask? Well, It's when they get released that the problems get bad. Their dangling strings can entangle animals of all types, and those balloony bodies doom any creature who mistakes a balloon for a meal.

We were figuring out a way to stop the balloon release
when our not-so-bright pelican pal Boris decided **he** would stop it...
with a poop bomb.

BULLSEYE!!

We were too late! All we could do was watch as the balloons floated up, up, up.

Until Mazi's heroic hound, Buttercup, leapt into action...

It was our bird, Roboto, riding our remote control plane!

While Roboto screeched his heroic war cry, Mazi was below, piloting the plane toward its target. Lucky was saved!

Following Roboto's lead,
the entire bird crew joined in on the hunt.
Exploding balloons and squawks
filled the skies!

Then from out of nowhere
two young dolphin troublemakers
snatched the biggest balloon!

We dove after them,
but they went deeper,
and deeper,
and deeper...

My headlamp revealed the dolphins ahead,
wrestling over the balloon as they entered
the remains of a shipwreck.

We got to the wreck just as the dolphins
were rocketing back to the surface...
but without the balloon?!

To find it, I had to go into that ships skeleton...

alone.

I searched until my light was dim and my air was low. Suddenly, twin eyes reflected back from under a chest's cracked lid, followed by tentacled arms, tightly clutching the string of the balloon.

Mine!

A magnificent giant Pacific octopus, and she had no intention of giving up her new balloon treasure.

I tried explaining to her how dangerous balloons were to her kind, how thousands of animals wash up each and every year, victims of balloons.

I was never happier to reach the surface!
As the sun set on another adventure filled day,
we headed home proud to be MicroActivists
who make every day a safer one for the
critters we love.

Together, we kids have the power to help make the planet a safer place for the wonderful critters we share it with, and that's just what we're doing!!

Want to learn what it is to become a MicroActivist and stand with us in protecting our planet? Of course you do!
Come visit our site and see what we are up to!!

www.MicroActivist.org

A big special THANKS goes out to all the MicroActivist supporters who believe in our efforts and who came together to help us bring this first book to kids everywhere. The story and imagery within these pages will entertain and inspire children to do their part in protecting our ocean.

Mazi and I would also like to extend a super sized heartfelt THANK YOU to all the good people at Lush who graciously believed in us enough to provide thesupport that allowed us to start on this journey full steam.

Making a book that meets the visual scale and grandure creative kids like us can muster is a tall undertaking. It was only through the combined effort of many highly skilled artists that our story was transformed into the visual treat you see on these pages. A big THANK YOU goes out to all these artists that contributed their time and wonderous creations...

Shawn Berryhill - Design, Direction, Illustation, Scene Creation & Final Assembly
Simona Ceccarelli - Character, Concept & Cover Design, Full Scene Illustrations
Steve Merghart- Character and Background Design. Technical Artist
Eric Lynx Lin - Concept Design and Technical Art Experimentation
James Graham - Technical Art Consultant and friend
Malcus Pine - Connor Character and Gear Creation
Songna@CartoonFactory - Core Model & Scenes, Rigging
Motion Cow - Pelican, Flying pigeon models
Baris Sahin - Sperm Whale Concept Design
Inspired Grafix - Whale Saddle & Gear
3d_molier - Sperm Whale base model
VisualCenter - Parakeet Head
Triduza - Parakkeet Body
Thibsert - Aviator Helmet
doncha-magoso - Pigeon Helmet
Massimo Righi - Bull Mastiff Base Model
MatvezhIvanovich - Base Octopus Model
3d_molier International - Dolphin base Character
Cadnav - Dog & Pigeon base models and other elements
PBR Game ready - Treasure Chest Scene
narkr - Ridgid Inflatable Watercraft
truf-design - Seaside Cliff Details
kenzuyee-1 - Seaside Cliff
Elena_Shvets - Groom Tuxedo
SgwaYang - Bride Dress
bad-panda - Balloons
levdesign - Shipwreck
reisal - Wedding Crowd
Law - RC Toy Biplane
mik.a. -RC Transmitter
rubykamen -Tablet

About Mazilyn

She may still be small, but my sister is one go-getter powerhouse of a little person! Mazi is my best friend. I know she has my back, and there's nothing I wouldn't do to protect her. With all the adventuring we do together, we kind of have to be tight. More than once we've held a barf bag for each other, huddled in shipboard bunks during rough crossings.

Sure we squabble, because we see things differently. But we're finding it's these differences that become our biggest strengths as we learn to work together.

Routine and consistency...those are not my things. But with Mazi's daily diligence, the animals we work hard to rescue snooze with full bellies.

Mazi is shaping up to be a really gifted photographer and filmmaker, and we look forward to seeing what she creates!

About Connor

Experts say I'm atypical, but who's really "typical" anyways? So I'm happy just being me. People say I'm already a pretty good storyteller for a youngster. The physical writing part can be tough, but Mom and Dad make for good note-takers. Guess what else parents are good for? Yup! Ample love and support that lifts me when I'm in doubt. We're a really tight tribe, and crazy adventuring, it's our gig!

Since I can't live underwater... yet... we find other ways to make do. Dad and I are building a submarine... well, actually Mom's making us stick to remote-controlled subs until we can prove they won't flood.

I also love rescuing animals. My sister and I ganged up to turn our home into a critter rescue for all the animals too injured to go back into the wild.

Nothing feels worse than finding a critter that was hurt by humans. I struggle to understand how people can harm other living creatures, It just feels wrong. I know it's going to take time for humanity to break free from these habits... but for me, that time can't come soon enough.

Made in the USA
Coppell, TX
21 May 2021